The
SPECIALITY,
GENERALITY,
and
PRACTICALITY
of the Church Life

Witness Lee

LIVING STREAM MINISTRY
Anaheim, California • www.lsm.org

First Edition, April 1984.

ISBN 978-0-87083-121-8 (softcover)
ISBN 978-0-87083-122-5 (hardcover)

Published by

Living Stream Ministry
2431 W. La Palma Ave., Anaheim, CA 92801 U.S.A.
P. O. Box 2121, Anaheim, CA 92814 U.S.A.

Printed in the United States of America

13   14   15   16   17   18   /   13   12   11   10   9   8   7

CONTENTS

FOREWORD

The chapters of this book are messages given during a time of training in the summer of 1971 in Los Angeles, California. They cover the speciality, generality, and practicality of the church life. The speciality of the church life is the faith (Rev. 14:12; Gal. 1:23; 2 Tim. 4:7), which is composed of the beliefs concerning the Bible, God, Christ, the work of Christ, salvation, and the church. Every real Christian shares the same beliefs regarding this common faith (Titus 1:4), our Christian faith. This faith is unique and is the ground of all the believers' genuine oneness. When the Body of Christ is divided, it loses everything; yet it has been divided again and again, mainly due to the overemphasis of certain beliefs other than those comprising the faith. Beliefs other than those comprising the faith have much disagreement and disputation. These beliefs may even become winds of teaching (Eph. 4:14) blowing us away from the oneness of the faith (v. 13).

Concerning the faith we must be very specific and particular (Jude 3; 1 Tim. 6:12); however, concerning the other things we must follow Paul's example and be general, never insisting that others believe as we do (Rom. 14:1-8). To possess such a spirit of generality is the generality of the church life. If we are special and insist on anything other than the common faith, the oneness will surely be damaged, and divisions will occur.

The primary thing, the first thing, in the practicality of the church life is life and the growth in life. For the experience and enjoyment of life we need to feed on Jesus (John 6:35, 57). The best way to eat and partake of Him, who is life, is to exercise our spirit by calling on His name and pray-reading His Word. The practicality of the church life also includes ministering the healthy teaching, the healthy word, all the saints prophesying in the meetings, practicing brotherly love, exercising obedience without any practice of human lordship, being a functioning member, and practicing the universal priesthood. Furthermore, it includes imparting life to others to bring them forth as fruit, caring for others by feeding and nourishing them, and spreading the Lord's testimony through migration.

Those of us who were in the meetings when these messages were released can never forget their timeliness and impact. The vision of all these points was deeply wrought into us. As the Lord is continuing to spread His recovery throughout the whole earth, this book, we believe, will fulfill a vital need and will be of immense practical help to all the local churches. We are grateful that this word can be made available to all the Lord's children in every place at this time. Also, we pray that He will grant such a reality in all the local churches.

Irving, Texas   Benson Phillips
July 1983

CHAPTER ONE

THE SPECIALITY OF THE CHURCH LIFE

(1)

Scripture Reading: Eph. 4:13-16; Gal. 1:23; 2 Tim. 4:7; 1 Tim. 6:12; Jude 3, 24; Acts 6:7; 13:8; 14:22; Gal. 3:25; 6:10; 1 Tim. 1:19; 3:9; 4:1, 6; 5:8; 6:10, 21; 2 Tim. 3:8; Titus 1:13; Rev. 14:12

In this book I have the burden to cover the speciality, generality, and practicality of the church life. In this chapter I will begin to cover the speciality of the church life. We all must know what it is in the church life that is so special.

THE FAITH

The speciality of the church life is *the faith*. In the New Testament the word *faith* is used with two different meanings. First, it means the action of believing (Rom. 5:1; Eph. 2:8; Heb. 11:1). We have faith in the Lord Jesus, and this is the action of believing. This is the subjective meaning of the word *faith*. There is also the second meaning, that is, the objective meaning of the word *faith*. *Faith* used in this way refers to the things in which we believe, the object of our faith, our belief (Titus 1:4; Rev. 14:12; 2 Tim. 4:7). So when we say that the speciality of the church life is the faith, we mean the faith that is the object of our believing. This is what we call our Christian faith. As Christians we have a unique faith.

Paul said that he fought the good fight and kept the faith (v. 7), and he also charged Timothy to fight the good fight of the faith (1 Tim. 6:12). Jude told us to contend for the faith once for all delivered to the saints (Jude 3). The faith mentioned in these verses does not mean our believing action but refers to the things in which we believe for our salvation and for the church life. All the verses listed at the beginning of this chapter are related to this. Thus, the faith is something unique, something specific, something special. Therefore, in the church life we have only one thing that is specific or special. That is *the faith,* our Christian faith, which is composed of the beliefs concerning the Bible, God, Christ, the work of Christ, salvation, and the church.

Concerning the Bible

The Bible is the Word of God. We believe that the Bible, word by word, is divinely inspired by God (2 Pet. 1:21), as the breath of God (2 Tim. 3:16). The genuine Christians do not have any doubt about this point. We must believe that the Bible is God's infallible Word.

Concerning God

God is uniquely one but triune, the Father, the Son, and the Spirit (Matt. 3:16-17; 28:19; 2 Cor. 13:14; Eph. 2:18; 3:14-17; Rev. 1:4-5). The Godhead is distinctively three, but They are not three Gods separately. In the Old Testament and in the New Testament, the Bible tells us definitely that God is one (Deut. 4:35, 39; Psa. 86:10; 1 Cor. 8:4; 1 Tim. 2:5).

Among the Christians there are some who believe that the Father is one person and the Son is another person, but the Spirit is just a power. Others believe that the three of the Godhead—the Father, the Son, and the Spirit—are three separate Gods. These concepts, strictly speaking, are heretical. We all have to believe that, according to the divine revelation of the holy Word, our God is uniquely one.

We have only one God, who is triune. Yet we are unable to define Him thoroughly because our mentality is so limited. Actually, we cannot even define ourselves very well. We know that we have a spirit, a soul, and a heart, but it is hard to define them. How then could we define the Triune God so thoroughly? We could only believe what is clearly revealed in the holy Word; that is, God is one but triune. This is the second item of our Christian faith.

Concerning Christ

Christ was the very God in eternity (John 1:1) and became a man in time (v. 14). His deity is complete, and His humanity is perfect. Hence, He is both God and man (20:28; Rom. 9:5; John 19:5; 1 Tim. 2:5), possessing both divinity and humanity. As a man He was anointed by God with the Spirit (Matt. 3:16; John 1:32-33; Luke 4:18-19) to accomplish God's eternal purpose. Hence, He is the Christ, the anointed One (Matt. 16:16; John 20:31). He is the Son of God (v. 31), who is the image of God (Col. 1:15), the effulgence of God's glory and the impress of His substance (Heb. 1:3), existing in the form of God and equal with God (Phil. 2:6; John 5:18); all the fullness of the God-head dwells in Him bodily (Col. 2:9). Thus, He is God Himself (Heb. 1:8).

As the Son of God He came in the flesh with (Gk., *para,* "from with") the Father (John 6:46) and in the name of the Father (5:43); hence, He is called the Father (Isa. 9:6). He was with God, and He was God in eternity past (John 1:1-2), not only coexisting but also coinhering with the Father all the time (14:10a, 11a; 17:21). Even while He was in the flesh on the earth, the Father was with Him (16:32). Hence, He and the Father were one (10:30), working in the Father's name and with the Father (v. 25; 14:10b), doing the Father's will (6:38; 5:30), speaking the Father's word (3:34a; 14:24), seeking the Father's glory (7:18), and expressing the Father (14:7-9).

As the eternal God He is the Creator of all things (Heb. 1:10; John 1:3; Col. 1:16); and as man who came in the flesh (1 John 4:2) with the physical blood and flesh (Heb. 2:14), He is a creature, the Firstborn of all creation (Col. 1:15b). Hence, He is both the Creator and the creature.

As the Sender and the Giver of the Spirit (John 15:26; 16:7; 3:34b), whom the Father sent in His (the Son's) name (14:26), the Son, being the last Adam in the flesh, became the life-giving Spirit through death and resurrection (1 Cor.

15:45b; John 14:16-20), who received all that is of the Son (16:14-15) to testify concerning the Son and glorify the Son (15:26; 16:14) and who is the breath of the Son (20:22). Hence, He is also the Spirit (2 Cor. 3:17) to abide coexistingly and coinheringly with the Son and the Father in the believers (John 14:17, 23; Rom. 8:9-11) to be the Triune God who is Spirit (John 4:24) mingled with the believers as one spirit (1 Cor. 6:17) in their spirit (Rom. 8:16; 2 Tim. 4:22). Eventually, He became the seven Spirits of God (Rev. 1:4; 4:5), who are the seven eyes of the Son, the Lamb (5:6).

As God becoming man, He is our Savior (Luke 2:11; John 4:42) by the name of Jesus—Jehovah our Savior, our salvation (Matt. 1:21). As the Lamb of God slain on the cross and shedding His physical blood for our sin and sins, He is our Redeemer (John 1:29; 1 Pet. 2:24; Heb. 9:26, 28; 1 Pet. 1:18-19). As the ascended Christ He is the Lord of all (Acts 2:36; 10:36), the Head over all things (Eph. 1:22), the Head of the church (Col. 1:18), and the Lord of lords and King of kings (Rev. 19:16).

In resurrection He is our life (Col. 3:4), the One who lives in us (Gal. 2:20), and God's power and wisdom to us to be our righteousness, sanctification, and redemption (1 Cor. 1:24, 30). Thus, in Him all the attributes of God become our virtues, and He is the contents, the all in all, of the new man (Col. 3:11).

Thus, we see that Christ is all: God, man, the Creator, the creature, the Father, the Son, the Spirit, the Savior, the Redeemer, the Lord, the Head over all, the Head of the church, the Lord of lords, and the King of kings. As such a One He is our life, righteousness, sanctification, redemption, and all in all. Praise Him!

Concerning the Work of Christ

Christ first became a man in incarnation (John 1:14) and died on the cross for our redemption (1 Pet. 2:24; Rev. 5:9). Then He rose from the dead for our regeneration (1 Pet. 1:3), ascended to the heavens to be the Lord of all (Acts 2:33, 36; 10:36), and will come back as the Bridegroom to the church

(John 3:29; Rev. 19:7) and the King of kings to all the nations (v. 16). These are the main aspects of the work of Christ. These aspects include His incarnation, His crucifixion, His resurrection, His ascension, and His coming back. No genuine Christian has any argument about these aspects of the work of Christ.

Concerning Our Salvation

A sinner must repent to God (Acts 2:38; 26:20) and believe in Christ (John 3:16; Acts 16:31) for forgiveness of sins (10:43), for redemption (Rom. 3:24), for justification (Acts 13:39), and for regeneration (John 3:6) in order that he may have the eternal life (v. 36) to become a child of God (1:12) and a member of Christ (1 Cor. 12:27). This is our salvation by God through faith (Eph. 2:4-9).

Concerning the Church

The church, composed of all the genuine believers in Christ, as the Body of Christ (1:22-23; Col. 1:24), is universally one (Eph. 4:4), and a local church as the expression of the Body of Christ is locally one—one city, one church (Rev. 1:11).

THE SPECIALITY OF THE CHURCH LIFE

These are the six main items of the proper Christian faith. All real Christians do not have any disputations about these items. Some may disagree with the point concerning one city, one church, but as a proper Christian we have to believe that the church is both universally one and locally one. As the Body of Christ, the church is universally one; as the expression of the Body of Christ, a local church is locally one. This does not mean, however, that a real believer in Christ who does not agree with one city, one church is not saved. He or she is saved, but there is something lacking, not for salvation but for the proper church life.

The faith is the speciality of the church life. This is something very specific, very special. Concerning these points of our Christian faith there should be no argument. If we are going to fight for something, we have to fight for this. There is no need for us to fight for other things. We have to fight the good fight of such a faith (1 Tim. 6:12). We have to contend for such a faith (Jude 3). We have to teach and preach such a faith.

THE WIND OF TEACHING

When Paul, who was then called Saul, was persecuting the church, he was attempting to destroy this faith. However, the Lord caught him, and he then became a preacher of the faith which formerly he ravaged (Gal. 1:23). Our fighting must be for this faith. We have to differentiate this faith from other kinds of teaching. Ephesians 4:13 says, "Until we all arrive at the oneness of the faith," and then in verse 14 there is the wind of teaching. In these two verses there is the faith, and there is teaching. The keeping of the Sabbath and circumcision are teachings. Head covering is a certain kind of teaching. Foot-washing is another kind of teaching. Sprinkling or immersion is also another kind of teaching. There is also the eating and drinking of Christ, pray-reading, tongue-speaking, and divine healing, as well as other kinds of teachings and practices. We should not think that any of these teachings or practices are included in the speciality of the church life.

What time should we have the Lord's table, morning or evening? This is a kind of teaching. How many times should we have the Lord's table, once a week or every day? This is also a kind of teaching. Should we use leavened bread or unleavened bread? This is another kind of teaching. When one prays, should he shut his eyes, or should he lift up his eyes toward the heavens? This also is a type of teaching. All these are teachings and have much disputation.

DIVIDED BY TEACHINGS

During the last five centuries, since the time of Martin Luther and the Reformation, Christians have been divided by all kinds of teaching. The divisions have resulted almost totally from the overemphasis of the teachings. For example,

John Nelson Darby took the lead to say that all the miraculous, supernatural gifts are dispensationally over, but the so-called Pentecostal people and today's charismatic people believe that they are still here. Even among these Christians there are different beliefs. Some say that a person may be regenerated, but he could never be baptized in the Holy Spirit without speaking in tongues. Others even say that one cannot be regenerated without speaking in tongues. With the matter of divine healing, there are schools of opinion. Some, like George Müller, believe in divine healing, not in the way of the gifts but in the way of grace. In his autobiography he told us that when he was young, he was very weak, yet he lived for ninety-three years. He experienced the Lord's healing by grace, but the charismatic or Pentecostal believers say that healing is by the gifts.

Just the matter of what name to baptize people in has schools of opinion. Some say that we must baptize people in the name of the Father, of the Son, and of the Holy Spirit. Others say that we should baptize people in the name of the Lord Jesus Christ.

Concerning the rapture, there are different schools of teaching, such as pretribulation rapture, posttribulation rapture, and partial rapture. These are teachings. Not one of them is an item of the faith.

There have been teachings upon teachings, and all the Christians have been divided and are still being divided by the differing teachings. Among the Brethren today there are hundreds of divisions. They began from 1828 or 1829, and by 1919, according to a record that we read at that time, the statistics showed that within those ninety years the Brethren were divided into one hundred fifty divisions, mainly because of so many different teachings.

CARING ONLY FOR THE FAITH

All Christians are the same in the faith, but we may be very, very different in the teachings. Do you believe that we all will be the same in the teachings? When will that time be? I can hardly believe that any two of us could ever be absolutely the same in teaching. Then what shall we emphasize? Shall we emphasize the teachings? If so, we will become divisive and eventually will be divided. We should not emphasize the teachings but only our Christian faith. We can emphasize this because with the faith there is no argument. In the faith we have no problems. We all are the same.

THE NEED TO GROW

However, we all have been infected, influenced, damaged, distracted, and even divided by all kinds of teachings. Therefore, we need to grow, and as we grow, we will arrive at the oneness of the faith (Eph. 4:13). The more we grow, the less we emphasize the teachings. All the teachings are like toys. The more childish we are, the more we like to play with the toys of teaching. A full-grown man, especially a grandfather, has no interest in toys. The more mature we are, the less toys we have. So we all need to grow until we arrive at the unique oneness of the faith.

CHAPTER TWO

THE SPECIALITY OF THE CHURCH LIFE

(2)

Scripture Reading: John 17:21-23; Eph. 4:3; Rom. 15:5-6; 1 Cor. 1:10-13; 11:19; Gal. 5:20; Titus 3:10

In the last chapter we have seen that the speciality of the church life is our Christian faith. Our Christian faith is composed of the beliefs concerning the Bible, God, Christ, the work of Christ, salvation, and the church. According to the Bible, these points constitute the fundamental and sound faith. We should not take anything away from this faith or add anything to it. If we take something away, we will surely be divisive, and if we add something to it, we will also be divisive. Christians are the same only in this faith. To keep us from being divisive, we must only hold this faith, nothing more.

Hence, our Christian faith is the ground of all the believers' genuine oneness. The last night the Lord Jesus was on the earth, He offered a unique prayer (John 17). His prayer revealed the importance of the oneness of all His believers. Nothing is as important as the oneness. When the church is divided, this oneness is lost. Satan knows that oneness is the crucial thing, the strategic point. He also knows that as long as he can keep Christians divided, he is successful.

THE CHURCH'S DEGRADATION

The early apostles ministered to the church what they had been commissioned by the Lord. However, it was not long before the things that they had passed on to the church began to be lost. At the beginning, the church received all the right things. But from the last part of the first century, the church gradually began to lose these things. On the one hand, by the fourteenth century nearly everything that God had given and committed to the Body had been lost. On the other hand, within those fourteen hundred years, the so-called church had picked up many heretical, dark, and sinful things. Whatever the church lost was something given by the Head, and whatever the church picked up was something injected from Satan. Thus, this period of time, as history shows us, was the darkest time.

THE LORD'S RECOVERY

Then, at the beginning of the sixteenth century, the Lord raised up Martin Luther. Before him some others had been raised up. (Actually, throughout the previous fourteen centuries, there were some faithful saints raised up by the Lord to recover the lost truths.) These paved the way for the Reformation. It was at this time that the Lord started His recovery and recovered the first item, justification by faith. Since that time many things have been recovered, such as sanctification by faith, holiness by faith, the living of a life by faith, victory by faith, and many other items.

THE MORAVIAN BRETHREN

In the 1700s some of the dear saints who were in the Lord's recovery began to pay their attention to the church life. As a result, at this time in Europe, there were many kinds of Brethren meetings. In the eighteenth century, some brothers moved to Bohemia to be with Count Zinzendorf. Under his leadership, they began to practice the church life, and to some extent it was proper and also quite wonderful. John Wesley, after going to Bohemia and staying with these brethren for some time, said that if he had not been burdened for England, he would have stayed in Bohemia with them for the rest of his life.

THE BRITISH BRETHREN

The practice of the church life by the brothers in Bohemia was good, but in 1828 to 1829 some brothers from England under the leadership of John Nelson Darby began to meet. Their practice of the church life was a great improvement. D. M. Panton, a great writer fifty years ago, said that this movement was greater than the Reformation. It was quite powerful and extremely influential.

Before the Reformation, as history shows us, the Bible was shut up by the Roman Catholic Church. Through Martin Luther and the Reformation it was released. However, it was opened through these brothers. There were many great scholars and teachers of the Bible among them—John Nelson Darby, Benjamin Newton, C. H. Mackintosh, William Kelly, and others. Through these brothers the Bible became not only a released book but also an open book. Today's fundamental theology is based mostly upon the Brethren teachings.

Because these brothers were so much for the teachings, the teachings became a source of many divisions. The first division occurred not long after their beginning in 1828. It happened because of the different concepts held by John Nelson Darby and Benjamin Newton. They had a big disputation mainly over the Lord's second coming. Since that first division, hundreds of divisions have occurred among them. All of them were due to the different concepts regarding teachings.

At the beginning, the Brethren were very good in the matter of life, but later they were distracted from life to teachings. Due to this, as history shows us, the Lord was forced to react.

THE INNER LIFE

Due to the deadness of the Reformed churches and the Brethren, the Lord reacted in the following matters. First, the Lord raised up some dear saints in the matter of the inner life. One of them was Madame Guyon. She was among the Catholics and deep in the inner life. Then in the last century the Keswick Convention was founded, and all those in it were along the inner-life line. William Law, Andrew Murray, and Mrs. Penn-Lewis were also in this line.

EVANGELISM

In His reaction the Lord also raised up evangelists. Especially in the last century there were a good number of giant evangelists. In this country there were D. L. Moody, Charles Finney, and R. A. Torrey. In England there were C. H. Spurgeon and Hudson Taylor, the founder of the China Inland Mission. Also there was William Carey, who went to India. Many of the evangelists founded some kind of mission to send out the gospel. This all occurred outside the Brethren.

THE PENTECOSTAL MOVEMENT

Besides the inner-life line and the line of evangelism, beginning in the middle part of the last century, also from England, there was the Pentecostal movement. Because the Brethren were so dogmatic and legal, there arose a group of people who did not care for any legality. Within the Pentecostal movement there were dancers, holy rollers, and holy laughers.

The Brethren might say that these things are not scriptural. But many were saved and revived through the Pentecostal movement. In China I saw one who had smoked opium for forty years. No one could help him get rid of his addiction. As a result of one time of jumping, he opened himself to the Lord and got saved. A robber who even the government could not stop fell down and rolled for five minutes. As a result, he also got saved. I personally talked to this one, and he told me the story. He was not helped by any eloquent preaching or a nice sermon but by the wild things. All these—the inner life, evangelism, and the Pentecostal movement—were the Lord's reactions to the dead rituals and dead teachings.

THE PROPER CHURCH LIFE

Up to the beginning of the twentieth century, many things had been recovered: the Bible knowledge, the inner life, evangelism, and the Pentecostal gifts. However, there was still not a proper church life recovered in a full way.

Then in 1920 the Lord did a marvelous thing to raise up the recovery of the proper church life in China, mainly through the leadership of Brother Watchman Nee. Since 1920 until today, fifty-one years have passed, and of this time I have been in it for forty-seven years. Day by day I have seen things happen, and what I am now passing on to you is something of my realization as a result of seeing all the things.

Please do not listen to any other talk about Brother Nee. I was with him throughout the years, and he had many long, heart-to-heart talks with me. Today people spread all kinds of rumors that Witness Lee is different from Watchman Nee, particularly concerning the church. Please do not listen to these rumors. They are lies.

I have documented every chapter of the book *Further Talks on the Church Life,* giving the day, the month, the year, and the place where Brother Nee gave the messages, because a rumor was spread that he changed his concept about the church life after the Second World War. But all those messages were given from and after 1948.

I have never met a man who was so much for the church. In 1932 he was invited by the Southern Baptists in my province to hold a summer conference. After that time until his arrest in 1952, he was never invited by any denomination in China to speak to them. Why? It was because of the matter of the church. His burden, his ministry, was so much for the church, but most of the missionaries, missions, and denominations could not tolerate him because his teachings annulled the divisive ground of all the denominations. Today many Christians read and appreciate Brother Nee's books, but some Christian bookstores in this country will not carry any of his writings on the church. Yet Brother Nee's burden was so much for the church.

I have contacted a good number of Christian leaders, and I have read a good number of books. However, I have never met a person or read the writings of any person who knew the Lord as deeply and who was for the church as much as Watchman Nee. This is the reason that I have been and am still one with him. I realized that he was the person raised up by the Lord for His specific purpose of recovering the proper church life.

The recovery of the proper church life, as was pointed out by Brother Nee, is the recovery of the unique oneness and the reality of the church. In the book *Further Talks on the Church Life,* he spent much effort to illustrate and show us the genuine oneness of the church. Chapter 4 of this book illustrates four kinds of unity, of which only one is the proper and genuine unity (oneness) of the church. This chapter is a classic. He also ministered very much of Christ as the reality and contents of the church.

GOD'S UNIQUE INTENTION

God's intention is to have a church, to have a Body for Christ. His intention is not just to have a number of saved people. Nor is it His intention merely to have a number of spiritual people or to have some fervent and godly Christians. God's unique intention is to have a church, to have a Body. All the previous items of recovery are for this ultimate item. The recovery of the church life is basically dependent on the recovery of the oneness and reality of the church. This is why oneness is the ultimate recovery of the Lord. Without oneness there is no proper ground for the church life.

In the past the Lord used different people to recover many items, yet the sad thing is that nearly every item of the recovery caused a division. All the items of the recovery should be for the church, but the people who have been used by the Lord to recover the items built up some division with that respective item of recovery. Those opposing the recovery of the church are not indifferent Christians but they are so much for the knowledge of the Bible, so much for the inner life, so much for evangelism, and so much for Pentecostal, charismatic things.

The target of much of the opposition is the oneness as the ground of the church life. Satan always does his best to damage this oneness. All the arrows will turn toward one who is for this oneness. Today Satan, the subtle enemy, hardly attacks spirituality, holiness, or any kind of charismatic things; he mainly attacks one thing—the genuine oneness as the ground of the church, which is the recovery of the practical church life.

THE TEACHINGS
AND THE PENTECOSTAL AND CHARISMATIC THINGS

I do not oppose the Pentecostal gifts or the emphasis of certain teachings, yet I am not for either. I do not oppose anything that is genuine. Why then am I not for these things? Let me illustrate. Suppose a factory has a choice of different materials to be used to make its product. Each of the different materials may be good, but the foreman knows from experience which material will make the best product. In the same manner, as a result of experience, I can tell you that the best way to build up a local church is to help the saints realize their human spirit and exercise their spirit to contact the Lord. By this way they will experience and enjoy the Lord, have the growth in life, and be preserved in the oneness as the ground of the church life. This does not mean that there is not another way to build up the church. There are other ways, but none is as good and proper as this way.

A local church might be built up by teaching, but if you use it as the basic way to build up a local church, you will suffer some loss. Also, a church might be built up by the Pentecostal and charismatic things, but if you use them as the basic way to build up a local church, you will suffer even greater loss.

A PERSONAL TESTIMONY

About thirty-seven years ago, a dear brother, who was very much for tongue-speaking, came and had a thorough talk with me. During our fellowship I pointed out to him the real situation in China. Among the Christians in China at that time, there were some prevailing ones, but none of the prevailing Christian preachers and ministers spoke in tongues. Watchman Nee never spoke in tongues. He definitely disagreed with the teaching that tongues are the unique manifestation of the baptism of the Spirit. Yet today Brother Nee's teachings have become so prevailing, not only among Chinese-speaking Christians but also throughout the whole world. Another prevailing one in China, Dr. John Sung the evangelist, also never spoke in tongues. He was strongly against anything Pentecostal.

Then I fellowshipped a second point with him. At that time two counties in China were full of Christians. One county, located in the province of Chekiang, was strongly against Pentecostalism. The other county that was in my home province was very much for the Pentecostal things. However, at the time of our talk, that Pentecostal work was nearly dried up, and the work in Chekiang that was against anything Pentecostal was prevailing. I told the brother that I do not mean that Pentecostal things are useless, but this situation proves that there is something better.

Then finally I pointed out to the brother that his Pentecostal group in our town had been meeting for a number of years yet still did not have over a hundred people. Our meeting place was very close to theirs, yet our number had been increasing all the time. He was a faithful believer, and after I had spoken to him, he added that he also realized that the brothers and sisters with him lived a careless and worldly life, but the brothers and sisters with us were so much with the Lord.

Today in Taiwan no other work has become as prevailing as the work of the local churches. In Taiwan there are seminaries, people with doctor's degrees, missionaries, fundamental people, and Pentecostal people, but no Christian work has ever become as prevailing as the local churches.

THE ATTITUDE OF THE WRITERS
OF THE NEW TESTAMENT TOWARD THE GIFTS

In the New Testament we see the gifts, but we have to consider the whole New Testament. In the book of Acts we see that Paul was powerful in divine healing during his early ministry (Acts 14:9-10; 19:11-12) though he did not stress it, but in his latter ministry, when his spiritual son, Timothy, had stomach trouble, he only told him not to drink water but to drink a little wine (1 Tim. 5:23). Also, Paul's intention in writing 1 Corinthians was to restrict the saints a little, or at least to adjust them, that they might use the tongues properly (14:6-11, 18-19). In Ephesians, the book on the church, Paul does not say anything about the miraculous gifts. In chapter 4 the gifts are persons. Paul knew that the best way to build up the church was not with teachings or with the gifts but by the Spirit with life.

In all his latter books—1 Timothy, 2 Timothy, and Titus—Paul did not say a word about the miraculous gifts. Furthermore, neither Peter nor John said anything in their books concerning the so-called Pentecostal gifts. Paul, Peter, and John were persons full of experience, yet none of them stressed the Pentecostal gifts.

THE WAY OF LIFE

The way of life by the Spirit is the profitable way. It goes very slow, but it is steady and steadfast. For the long run, nothing can beat this way. It goes on year after year, and it goes from place to place. It also becomes stronger and stronger, and it gets more and more solid. It is slow, but for the long run, it is the fastest way. It is like raising an orchard. The trees being grown for the production of fruit grow quite slowly, but for the long run, it is not slow. Eventually, the way of life by the Spirit produces something that nothing can shake or destroy.

A FINAL WORD

We should not oppose anything that is genuinely of the Bible. The local churches must be all-inclusive. However, whether in teaching or practice, it is wise to use the things that are better. When we come to the generality and the practicality of the church life in the forthcoming chapters, this will become more and more clear. So many things are not within the circle of the speciality, our Christian faith, but in the realm of the practicality, which is for practice. An example is pray-reading. We do not insist on pray-reading, because it is not an item of our Christian faith. But it is something for our practice. I believe that by fellowshipping in this way we all will become clearer and clearer.

CHAPTER THREE

THE GENERALITY OF THE CHURCH LIFE

(1)

Scripture Reading: Rom. 14:1-7, 12-21; 15:3-5; 1 Cor. 8:4-13; 10:25-29; 9:20-22; 7:7-8, 25-26; 1 Tim. 5:14

In this chapter we will begin to see the generality of the church life. In the church life we all must be general. However, before we can be general, we must be special. Concerning the six items of our Christian faith, we must be very specific, very particular. If we are general about it, we are wrong, but this is just one side. We need balance.

THE GENERALITY PRACTICED BY PAUL

As long as we have the solid foundation of the faith, the speciality, laid, we can be very, very general. The apostle Paul was such a person. He was general to such an extent that, according to the record in Acts 21, when he went to Jerusalem the last time, he was persuaded to go to the temple again and even to keep some of the regulations of Judaism. In Romans and Galatians he boldly spoke against Judaism, yet when he went to Jerusalem the last time, he was persuaded to go to the temple again.

Since Paul was a person who was faithful and strong, how could he take the advice to go back to Judaism and its priests, even paying the fee for four others? He was practicing generality. Of course, I will admit that on this occasion Paul went a little too far; even he was out of balance, so he made a mistake. Too much balance is still out of balance. He tolerated the situation, but this time the Lord did not. If Paul could have passed through those seven days without any trouble, that would have proved that what he did was right. But the Lord would not tolerate this in order to keep the truth of the gospel clear to the coming generations. However, this does show that Paul was a person who would be so general in the church life.

EATING THINGS SACRIFICED TO IDOLS

According to Paul's teaching, the New Testament teaching, should we as Christians eat things sacrificed to idols, or should we not eat them? If you say no, I would say that your answer is wrong. If you say yes, I would also say that your answer is wrong. I have some verses that give me the ground to tell you yes (1 Cor. 8:4-8; 10:25-27), and I also have some verses that give me the ground to tell you no (8:9-13; 10:28-29). In the New Testament there is no definite answer concerning this matter.

Not more than ten years ago did I get into the spirit of the writer of all these verses. Then I began to understand his meaning. It is not a matter of yes or no; it is a matter of generality. To say definitely that one should not eat anything offered to idols will cause problems. This will exclude some believers. However, to say yes will also cause trouble. It will cause more damage. So Paul was general.

We all have to learn to be balanced. You may feel that you have the freedom to eat anything. You feel that idols mean nothing (8:4-6), and every idol has been put under your feet. Even you can eat the things offered to the idol in front of the idol. But do you realize that your liberty and boldness will damage some weaker ones? They would never fellowship with you because they think that you are associated with idols. Hence, on some occasions Paul would say that we should eat, and on the other occasions he would say that we should not eat. Both are right.

PRACTICING THE GENERALITY

Suppose I am now fellowshipping, taking the Lord's table, with a certain group of believers, and all of them are so strong in their conscience. They might say, "We do not care for idols; they mean nothing." I will agree with them:

"Yes, praise the Lord, eat! Eat the things sacrificed to the idols. They mean nothing." I say yes to them. But when I am with another group where the dear ones are weak in their conscience, afraid of being associated with anything of the idols, they might say that they do not have the freedom to eat the things offered to idols. I also will agree with them: "No, you should not do it." Then you might rebuke me, saying that I am a person with two faces, because you heard me say yes to one group and no to another group. We can never experience and practice this without a spirit of generality. Without such a spirit we will surely cause division. It will not be possible for us to keep the oneness.

THE GENERAL ATTITUDE IN ROMANS 14

This is the reason that Paul took such a general attitude in Romans 14. He said that some eat everything; however, others who are weaker eat only vegetables (vv. 2-3). To these weaker ones all animals are dirty, and only vegetables are clean. Suppose a believer among us insists to eat only vegetables. What should we do? Probably we would contend for the "truth" that today is the day of grace, and we can eat everything. We would insist that he eat some slain animal day by day, signifying that the Lord died for our sins. Yet this dear one would say, "I do believe in the Lord's redemption. I thank the Lord that He was crucified for my sins, but my conscience will not allow me to take any meat." This is the problem today. Christians are divided because they lack a spirit of generality.

In Romans 14 there is also the matter of keeping days (vv. 5-6). Some regard one day as special. These regard the seventh day as the top day of the days. However, some regard all days alike. To these all days are the same. When I was young, I thought that Paul was sacrificing the truth. I said to myself, "Paul, how could you receive people who feel that today they have to keep the Sabbath? Why didn't you tell us definitely that to keep the Sabbath is wrong? Today is the day of grace. There is no need for us to keep the Sabbath. How can you say that it is okay?"

Suppose a brother of the Seventh-day Adventists begins to meet with us and insists on keeping the Sabbath. What would you do? We all have to learn the spirit of Paul in Romans 14. I have learned this lesson in a hard way. When I was young, I got the best teaching about immersion. Because of this, whenever I met another Christian, the first question I asked was, "By what way were you baptized?" If he said by immersion, I was happy. If he said by sprinkling, I would express my disapproval.

Also, in my early years when I met a Christian, I would check with him, "Do you believe in the Lord Jesus' coming back?" If he answered yes, then I would ask him when he would be raptured. If he said something not in agreement with me, I would show him many verses proving that what I believed was accurate. In a sense, those teachings that I was so fond of were my toys.

THE NEGLECT OF ROMANS 14

Today many Christians are talking about the Body in Romans 12, but nearly all of them have neglected Romans 14. Without Romans 14 we can never have the Body life. Most who are talking about the Body life do not have it; they only have division. Today the Lord's recovery is mainly of the oneness. If we are going to have the oneness, we have to become so general. When a brother who is a Seventh-day Adventist comes and insists on keeping the seventh day, we should say to him, "Brother, if you like to keep the Sabbath, you do it. If we have the time, we will come to be with you. We have no problem with you, and we have no argument." This is the attitude, the spirit, taken by Paul in Romans 14. But this does not mean that Paul was not clear about the teaching of the Sabbath. He was very clear, but he did not insist. We are clearly told by him in Colossians 2 that the Sabbath was a shadow of the Christ who was to come. The Sabbath was a shadow, and now that the body has come, the shadow is over. However, in Romans 14 Paul still tolerated it.

Also, when a brother comes and insists on only eating

vegetables, we should say to him that we have no problem with it. When he eats only vegetables, we eat vegetables with him. Again, this does not mean that Paul was not clear about the matter of eating foods. He was very clear, but he did not insist. Can we be so general?

THE MARRIAGE PROBLEM

Now we come to another point. In 1 Corinthians 7, concerning marriage, Paul's attitude was that it is better for the saints not to get married, to keep their virginity (vv. 7-8), and if they do not have a wife, to remain as they are (v. 27). He also said in verse 26, "I consider then that this is good because of the present necessity, that it is good for a man to be as he is."

This was Paul's attitude in 1 Corinthians. But if you go to his later writing, he says in 1 Timothy 5:14, "I will therefore that younger widows marry, bear children, keep house, give no opportunity to the opposer for reproach." In 1 Corinthians 7 he discourages people from getting married, yet in 1 Timothy 5 he encourages the young women to marry, bear children, and keep house. If Paul were here, we might ask him, "Brother Paul, where do you stand? Do you stand with 1 Corinthians 7 or 1 Timothy 5?"

Was Paul wrong? We cannot say this. It is up to the circumstances. If the circumstances are such that it is good for you to be single and love the Lord with all that you are, that is proper. However, the circumstances sometimes do not allow this. Rather, you need a wife or a husband with a family. If this is the case, then the young ladies should get married. It is the same in principle as with the matter of eating things sacrificed to idols. It is not a matter of yes or no. It is a matter that depends on the circumstances. You should not say yes; neither should you say no. There is nothing legal or definite. It should not be like what is practiced in the Roman Catholic Church. They have set up a regulation that all the nuns, monks, and priests should not marry. That is too legal.

We all have to realize from these cases that in a local

church, as far as all the teachings are concerned, we should not be so specific but general. However, as far as our Christian faith is concerned, we must be specific. Concerning the faith, we must be definite. But as for teachings such as immersion, sprinkling, head covering, foot-washing, eating, keeping days, marriage, and so many other things, we must be general. If we are not general, we will surely be divisive.

PRACTICING THE GENERALITY
TOWARD OTHER LOCAL CHURCHES

This is not only a principle for individuals; it is also the principle for all the local churches. We must not only be general toward individuals but also toward other churches. We should not be so definite. We should not be so set. Every local church must learn to follow all the other local churches. For example, the church in Los Angeles followed the church in San Francisco in the matter of pray-singing. Neither was pray-reading started in Los Angeles. The church in Los Angeles, as also a follower of the other churches, learned pray-reading from the church in Taipei and pray-singing from the church in San Francisco.

We do not know what will happen tomorrow in the church in one place or next week in the church in another place. There may be something new in a locality that will be so helpful to all the local churches. If so, all the churches should take it. We all have to learn to be general. We should not say that a certain way is the best way to practice the church life or that a certain way is the best way to have a local church. At the present time I and so many others feel that to exercise the spirit and to take care of the inner life by pray-reading and feeding on the Lord Jesus is the most profitable way for us to have the proper church life. But we are open to the Lord. We do not know how far the Lord will go on. We all have to admit that there is still a big field for us to explore. It may be that after two years something new will be discovered. We should not be so definite, so set. We should be open, and we should be general.

THE BETTER THINGS
FOR BUILDING UP A LOCAL CHURCH

In the last two chapters I pointed out that teachings are not so good for the building up of a local church. I also stated that neither are the gifts so good for the building up of a local church. There is something better—the exercise of the spirit, the growth in life, the pray-reading, and the feeding on the Lord. These are the better things for the building up of a local church. I do not mean that teachings are absolutely of no use; neither do I mean that gifts are absolutely of no use. We have seen that a good number of people were raised up by the gifts, and a good number of saints were edified by teachings. To say that teachings and the gifts are absolutely of no use is wrong. However, to build up the local church with life, with the growth in life, and with oneness is the better way. Nothing can surpass the way of life, the way of enjoying Christ for growth, and the way of oneness.

We should never try to adjust or correct other churches. If the church you visit were under your direction, you might do things differently. But when it is not under your direction, you should not do anything. It is the same as driving or riding in a car. When you ride with someone, you should never say a word. That is his car under his driving. But if the car is turned over to you, you may drive it another way. We should never be a back-seat driver.

The problem, however, is that when we visit another local church, we may tell the saints there that the practice in the local church where we are is the right way. We may try to make the church in another city like the church in our place. We should not do this. We should never say that the way in our church is the normal way. It is absolutely not right to correct others like this. Your way might be the worst. But even if it is the best, there is no need for you to try to convince others to take it. To try to convince others of your way will only cause division. If you think that your way is the best and it indeed is the best, others will see it and will learn of it. If others do not care to learn of it, that is up to them.

Never be bothered by something different from your concept. If you hold the concept that the meetings have to be quiet, yet you get into a meeting that is noisy, do not be bothered. You have to learn to be general and go along with it. If your concept is to have a noisy meeting, a meeting that is full of praisings, and you come to a meeting that is quiet, do not be bothered. Be quiet with them. Be general.

By all means we have to keep the oneness. Do not make anything definite. Do not make anything specific. Do not have anything set. We should be open, we should be general, and we should be learning all the time.

CHAPTER FOUR

THE GENERALITY OF THE CHURCH LIFE

(2)

Scripture Reading: Matt. 18:17; Rom. 16:17; 2 Thes. 3:6, 14; 1 Cor. 5:9-13; Titus 3:10; 2 John 9-11, 7

In the last chapter we saw that for the practice of the church life in oneness, the apostle Paul took such a general stand concerning teachings and practices. As to the matter of eating, whether a Christian brother eats this or another eats that, neither should criticize the other. As to the matter of keeping days, the principle is the same. Whether a Christian brother keeps a day and regards it as something special and another considers all days the same, neither should criticize the other. Everyone must be general.

Concerning the matter of eating things sacrificed to idols, Paul did not say yes or no; he only took care of the other's conscience. Also, concerning whether one should get married, it is difficult to say yes or no. It depends upon the circumstances. If someone can stand all kinds of situations, it may be better that he does not get married. If not, it is better for him to get married. It is general. Paul knew all the proper teachings, but in the practice of the church life he was so general. We all have to learn that to keep the oneness of the Body we must practice this generality. If we are special, if we are definite and specific in anything other than our faith, surely the oneness will be damaged. The oneness will be hurt, and then we will be divided. The main cause for the divisions among Christians is the neglect of caring for the generality of the church life.

THE BALANCE TO THE GENERALITY

Now we need to see another balance. We have seen that

the speciality is balanced by the generality. The generality also has to be balanced by something. We as human beings easily become one-sided and go to an extreme. In the book of Hosea in the Old Testament, there is a verse in which the Lord likened Ephraim to an unturned cake (7:8). Cakes baked in a pan need to be turned again and again. If the cakes are not turned, one side will be burned, and the other will remain raw. Some of the children of Israel were like an unturned cake in the eyes of the Lord. They were always one-sided, and this is still the problem with the Lord's children today. So many Christians are like unturned cakes. This is why we had to see the balance to the speciality in the last chapter and why in this chapter we must see another balance. In a later chapter we will see another balance. We need to be turning all the time. Then we will be the best "cake." The speciality needs the generality to balance it. The generality also needs something to balance it.

At the beginning of this chapter I listed all the verses in the New Testament regarding the persons who cannot and should not be received into the church life. Do not think that the church has to practice the generality to the degree that it has to take all kinds of persons. No, not at all. Yes, we should be general, but still there are certain persons with whom we cannot be general, nor with whom we should be general.

ONE WHO NEGLECTS TO HEAR THE CHURCH

In Matthew we can see the seriousness of neglecting to hear the church (18:15-17). We think that if one loses his temper, it is something serious, or if one commits something immoral, it is more serious. However, if someone neglects to hear the church, we consider it almost as nothing because we do not have a church-consciousness. However, the Lord Jesus said that we have to consider such a one as a Gentile. In the Bible a Gentile is worse than a sinner. The Lord Jesus also said that we have to consider such a one as a tax collector. We should not consider him as a kind of weak brother and sympathize with him. Not to hear the church is serious.

The Roman Catholic Church exercised too much authority over the saints, so an item of the Reformation was to attack this over-exercise of authority. Thus, most of the Christians are so liberal concerning the church. Almost no one respects the church today. When we talk about respecting the church, some people even condemn us, saying that this is Catholicism and that this is the setting up of a pope. To have a pope is surely wrong. To exercise too much authority over the saints is also seriously wrong, but this does not mean that the church has no authority, nor does it mean that we should not be church-conscious.

Let me illustrate this point. Suppose we have a brother who is nice in many ways. But he does something to a brother who is rough and not so nice. Eventually, three brothers are forced to tell the church about it. The elders would then advise him to repent and to apologize to the rough brother. Yet he would not listen; rather, he would say that the rough brother was wrong. According to today's Christian concept, this is not so serious. Some might even say that it was the rough brother's fault, not the fault of the nice one. Others might even sympathize with him based upon the fact that he has been so nice all the time.

What should we do in such a case? Would you agree to consider him as a Gentile and as a tax collector? I believe most Christians would not take this as something serious. Some would side with the nice brother and say that we should not make an issue of it. Others would say, "Let time vindicate. Probably after two weeks everything will be fine, and they will be reconciled one to another. Forget about it for the present time." These attitudes are held by most Christians because they are not church-conscious. They do not consider that to neglect to listen to the church is exceedingly serious. Even though in the church life we must be general, certain ones in some things might not respect the church or listen to it. In this matter we cannot be general. This is altogether something of the oneness of the church. We must be conscious of the oneness.

THOSE WHO CAUSE DIVISIONS

Romans 16:17 says, "I exhort you, brothers, to mark those who make divisions and causes of stumbling contrary to the teaching which you have learned, and turn away from them." This verse can only be applied where the church life is proper. If a Christian group is divisive already, it does not have the standing to use this verse. It must practice the church life with the proper and balanced teachings of the apostle Paul—the tempered teachings, not the untempered teachings. To use this verse, a local church must be properly balanced. Otherwise, what it teaches will not be proper, and it will be hard for a believer to listen to that church. Every local church must be very careful not to overemphasize anything outside the realm of the faith.

Let me illustrate this point. Suppose a local church over-emphasizes head covering, telling everyone that head covering is a specific thing in the church life, and all the sisters must have their head covered. If this is done, some of the sisters might become dissenting. Then someone might say, "Let us apply Romans 16:17 to them." This would be a wrong application because the church is wrong in overemphasizing head covering. The overemphasis of head covering is what caused the dissension.

Now let us consider a further point. Suppose a local church stresses the oneness, the unity. It stresses one city, one church all the time. One city, one church even becomes the church's slogan. As a result, some of the saints become dissenting, even undermining the church by going from member to member and saying, "This is really too much. The church here is a one city, one church sect. It is a local-church sect." If this is the case, Romans 16:17 has to be applied to the dissenting saints. This is the same in principle as with our Christian faith when we say that the Bible is God's Word, divinely inspired word by word. Regardless of how much we say this, it does not mean that we overemphasize it. Day by day we may say this, yet still we are not overemphasizing it, because this is something specific in our Christian faith. But suppose someone says, "Only say that the word of the Bible is inspired by God. Do not emphasize word by word. Just take the Bible in a general way. The Bible is good, but probably some of the verses, at least some of the words, are not inspired by God. Some are only spoken by the writers themselves." In such a case we must apply Romans 16:17.

We must be clear and exceedingly balanced. According to history, being unbalanced, overemphasizing certain things, is the cause of all divisions. The apostle Paul's teaching was very much balanced, so he could say that anyone who causes division contrary to his teaching has to be avoided, has to be turned away from, has to be marked out. However, in some of the so-called churches, this verse could never be applied, because they do not have the standing to apply it. They are a division already. To apply this verse we must absolutely not be divisive. We must fully be a genuine, proper local church with much balance.

In 2 Thessalonians 3:6 and 14 the principle is the same as in Romans 16:17. Paul says that some walk disorderly and not according to the things which were handed down and received from him. He also says that if anyone does not obey his word in this Epistle, we should mark this one so as not to mingle with him. We should mark these, withdraw ourselves from them, and not mingle with them. To mingle with them will strengthen their divisive spirit. It will help them cause more dissension. Only a local church that is proper, genuine, and normal has the position to apply verses such as Romans 16:17 and 2 Thessalonians 3:6 and 14.

ONE WHO IS SINFUL

Now let us consider 1 Corinthians 5. These verses cover sinful things such as idolatry, fornication, reviling, drunkenness, and rapaciousness. All these things are exceedingly evil and either insult God's divinity or damage humanity. Idolatry is something that blasphemes the person of God. Fornication, reviling, drunkenness, and rapaciousness damage humanity. God cares very much for His divine person. He is a jealous God. He also cares for humanity. So God will not tolerate any of these things. No one who practices idolatry or is a fornicator should be allowed in the church life. The local church also should not tolerate any person who is a reviling one, a drunken one, or a rapacious one. All these things damage humanity and also damage the Lord's testimony on this earth among human beings. Therefore, Paul told us that a Christian brother or sister who practices any of these things has to be removed from among the church (v. 13). But as long as something is not sinful and as long as it is not related to idols, or to any kind of fornication, reviling, being drunken, or rapaciousness, we must tolerate it.

ONE WHO IS FACTIOUS

Then Titus 3:10 says clearly that a man who is factious after he is admonished once or twice, refuse, because division damages the Body of Christ. God takes care of Himself. He also takes care of humanity. Third, He takes care of the Body of Christ. In a local church none should do anything that damages God's person, humanity, or the Body of Christ. If one damages any of these, we cannot continue to receive him. Either the church has to put him away, refuse him, or turn away from him. We cannot mingle with such persons.

ONE WHO GOES BEYOND THE TEACHING OF CHRIST

Second John 9 says, "Everyone who goes beyond and does not abide in the teaching of Christ does not have God." This refers to one who goes beyond, goes further, than the teachings of the apostles concerning Christ. The apostles taught that Christ is the Son of God incarnated to be a man and that He is the One who gives us eternal life. They also taught that He is the One who died on the cross for our sins and was resurrected on the third day. These are the main points of the apostles' teaching. Giving eternal life is for regeneration. Dying on the cross for our sins is for redemption. Resurrection is for life impartation.

Even in the first century, some so-called Christians, called antichrists, had gone beyond these points. Some said that Christ did not come in the flesh (v. 7). In other words, they did not recognize the incarnation of Christ. Today in the same principle some of the so-called modernists who call themselves Christians say that Christ died on the cross as a martyr, suffering persecution, and that He did not die there for our sins. These say that His death was not for redemption, only for martyrdom. They also say that Christ never resurrected. If one of those will admit that Christ was resurrected, he will say that He was only resurrected spiritually, not physically. All these persons have gone beyond the teaching concerning Christ.

We should not give this kind of antichrist or modernist a greeting (vv. 9-10). If we give them a greeting, we share in their evil works. Even the more, we should not receive them into our home. Someone might say that if we practice this, we are too specific and that we must be general. But we cannot be general with these kinds of persons. They are the ones who blaspheme Christ. We cannot mingle with blasphemers of the Lord. Anyone blaspheming the Lord Jesus must be put out of the church. We have to turn away from him.

I hope that this word has made it clear who are the persons with whom we cannot mingle. We Christians many times are specific when the Lord demands that we be general. Also, many times we are general when the Lord demands that we be specific. However, I believe that after pray-reading all these verses a few times, you will get the clear concept. In the church life, regardless of how general we are, there are certain persons whom we cannot receive. We have to be specific with these kinds of persons. We cannot mingle with any of them.

CARING FOR THE STANDING

Many times people have come to our meetings and have become excited. They proclaimed that our meetings are wonderful and that the way the Lord is moving among us is marvelous. However, after some days, they stopped coming because they heard something with which they disagreed. This kind of behavior shows that these dear ones had never seen what the oneness of the church is. If they had seen what the church is and what the oneness of the church is, they would not have cared about the things with which they disagreed. They would not have cared for the condition of the church but for the proper standing. Let me illustrate by using the captivity of the people of Israel as an example or as a kind of type. During the normal time in their history, all the Israelites in the Holy Land were one, taking Jerusalem as their unique center. Later on, they became scattered. In other words, they became divided. First, some were carried away to Assyria. Then some were carried away to Egypt. Eventually, nearly all the remaining ones were taken to Babylon. This was their captivity. This was also their division. After seventy years of captivity, the Lord commanded them to return. Not a large number, but only a small remnant, returned.

Nehemiah, Ezra, and Haggai show us that the returned ones were in a poor condition. Some had married Gentile wives. Suppose that in Babylon most of the remaining Hebrews were spiritual and godly, even having some giants of spirituality among them. Also, suppose that they always had good meetings. Furthermore, suppose that those in Syria and Egypt were not as good as those in Babylon but at least better than the returned ones. Now my question is this: "Which of these four groups would you join?" Suppose most of the people in Babylon were godly, spiritual, and lovable, and their meetings were high. Also many spiritual giants were there. Would you go to join them or the returned group in Jerusalem whose condition was so poor?

The real situation today is that almost no Christians take care of the standing. Most care only for the condition. Why do Christians like to join a particular group? It is because those in it are spiritual, or their meetings are good. However, we have to realize that the standing is much more important than the condition. The standing can never be changed, but the condition may fluctuate. Today the meeting may be marvelous, but tomorrow it may be poor. I do not say that we should not pay attention to our condition, but this is not the first thing. This is not the primary thing. It is secondary. The primary thing is the standing. If we have seen what the church is and what the recovery of the oneness is, we would care mainly for the standing and pay some attention to the condition.

We like to improve our condition, but our burden is for the position, the standing. The people in Babylon might have been quite spiritual. They might have had outstanding teachers expounding the law and ministering the Word properly and richly. However, regardless of how spiritual they were, how much they knew the Word, or how much they were behaving in the proper way, they were not in the oneness, and they did not rebuild the temple. They were not the ones to accomplish this because they did not have the standing. They might have even had the ability and the capability, but they still did not have the standing. Therefore, they could not rebuild the temple. God's desire on this earth is not mainly the spirituality of His people. His main desire is the rebuilding of His house.

History tells us that not long after the return from captivity and the building of the temple, Christ came the first time. He was born in Bethlehem, through a descendant of the house of David. Regardless of how spiritual those in Babylon were, they were not the people with the proper standing for Christ to be born through them. Christ was born in Bethlehem of one who was a descendant of the returned ones. Only the returned ones standing on the proper ground fulfilled God's purpose to rebuild the temple and to bring Christ to this earth. If one comes to take the way of the local churches, to be a part of the Lord's recovery, only because the meetings are good, I am afraid that someday he will leave, because the condition of the meetings will fluctuate. Today there is a clear sky, but tomorrow there may be a foggy sky, and the third day a stormy sky. Then he will be scared away. However, if he is clear about the standing, he will not care for the fluctuating weather.

A WORD OF SUMMARY

I encourage you to bring all these things to the Lord and

pray. Have you really seen the church? Have you really seen what the recovery of the oneness is? Throughout the past years we have passed through many kinds of sufferings, persecutions, attacks, and criticisms, not from the Gentile world but mainly from some in Christianity. By the Lord's mercy we have never been shaken. The more we are attacked, the more solid we become. The Lord has gained the victory.

We who have been brought back to "Jerusalem" have to be clear about what we are doing and where we are standing. Today the condition may be glorious, and tomorrow it may be pitiful. But do not be bothered by this. The third day may be wonderful. However, we need to stand in a balanced way. If we are not balanced, we will cause trouble. We will lose the impact and even allow some ground to be taken by the enemy. As long as we are standing on the proper ground with all the proper balances, we will be here until the Lord comes back. Nothing can surpass this way or this testimony.

CHAPTER FIVE

THE PRACTICALITY OF THE CHURCH LIFE

(1)

Scripture Reading: John 10:10b; 6:57, 63; 21:15; 1 Cor. 3:2, 6; 15:45b; 6:17; Eph. 4:13-15; 2:21; 1 Pet. 2:2-3, 5

In the foregoing chapter we pointed out that God is mainly for four things. First, He cares for Himself, His divine person. Second, He cares for humanity. Man was made by Him in His own image for His expression. Third, God cares for His Christ, His Son Jesus Christ. Finally, God cares for the Body of Christ.

God will not tolerate anything that is a blasphemy or insult to Himself. God refuses any idolatry or anyone who worships idols. He never allows any man to have another God. God also cares so much for the man that He made to express Him. Anything that damages humanity such as fornication, rapaciousness, or things like this, God will never allow. Then anything that insults the person of Christ or the redemptive work of Christ, including His incarnation, His crucifixion, His resurrection, His ascension, His lordship, or His coming back, God will never tolerate. The Body of Christ, the church, is uniquely one; nothing should divide it or damage it. Anything that damages it, God will never allow. This is why the apostle said to admonish a factious man once, at the most twice, but if he will not listen, reject him (Titus 3:10). God is so strong regarding this point because to be factious damages the Body of Christ. God cares for these four things.

Some Christians, however, believe and teach that God cares so much for what they call the "great commission," that is, to go preach the gospel and then baptize people by immersion. Others believe and teach that God cares so much for the speaking in tongues. Among these people some teach that if you do not speak in tongues, you cannot receive the baptism of the Holy Spirit. However, God has reacted to these kinds of teachings. Many good saints have never been baptized by immersion. Also, thousands have been saved who never spoke in tongues. Even so many became spiritual giants. During the last half century, almost no one was as prevailing as Brother Watchman Nee, but he never spoke in tongues. A number of others who were used by the Lord, such as Charles H. Spurgeon, D. L. Moody, R. A. Torrey, and George Müller, did not speak in tongues.

However, this does not mean that tongue-speaking is wrong. Neither does it mean that immersion is wrong. I am for immersion. My point is that God does not care as much for the different teachings and practices as some Christians do.

LEARNING A BASIC LESSON

We all must learn a basic lesson. If a person is an idol worshipper, he could never be used by God. Rather, God refuses anyone who worships an idol. God also refuses a fornicator. He could never use such a one. However, you cannot say that God will refuse someone who does not agree with immersion. You may be through with him, but God is not through with him.

Also, we cannot say that God could use a modernist, one who says that Christ is not the Son of God or says that Christ did not die on the cross for our sins but only suffered martyrdom. Neither can God use one who is factious. God refuses such persons. But you cannot say that if one does not speak in tongues, God is through with him. You may be through with him, but God is not through with him.

God's primary consideration is that as long as you love and worship Him as your unique God, as long as you love humanity and do nothing to damage it in any manner, such as fornication and rapaciousness, as long as you honor Christ, respect Him, receive Him, follow Him, love Him, and take

Him as your Redeemer, as your life, as your Lord, and as your everything, and as long as you love the Body of Christ, the church, and live for it, you will be a person whom God will use very much.

All the other things are minor. If you like to wear a head covering, you can cover your head for the Lord's sake. If you like foot-washing, you may practice it. If you like to take small pieces of leavened bread for the Lord's table, do it. If you like to take unleavened bread, prepare some. We should not oppose any teachings and practices like these. However, if I am asked to prepare the bread, I will prepare something unleavened. I do not insist on unleavened bread, yet I practice it. If I were a sister, surely I would wear a head covering. According to my conscience, I would have to cover my head. I would practice these things in this manner, yet I do not insist on any way. God's basic consideration and caring is only for Himself, for humanity, for Christ, and for the Body of Christ, the church.

LIFE—THE PRIMARY THING
IN THE PRACTICALITY OF THE CHURCH LIFE

Now we come to the last matter, the practicality of the church life. This is also something that we have learned from history. Although we were not able to be in so many things during the past twenty centuries, we have been able to study history, including biographies and autobiographies of many Christians. By reading these books, we have come to know about the different practices among Christians during the last nineteen hundred years. As a result, we realize that today the best thing, the primary thing, the first thing, that we have to take care of in the practicality of the church life is the matter of life.

The history of the Lord's recovery shows that in the past four or five hundred years almost all the teachings have been recovered. Also, the gifts have been recovered to the uttermost and even to the extreme. However, the matter of life has never been adequately recovered.

THE INNER-LIFE LINE

In the history of the Lord's recovery, there is an aspect that has been called the inner-life line. It began with the mystics about three hundred years ago. The epistle to the church in Sardis in Revelation 3 refers prophetically to the church during the time of the Reformation. To the church in Sardis the Lord said, "You have a name that you are living, and yet you are dead. Become watchful and establish the things which remain" (vv. 1-2). This means that what still remains has to be made alive. In the eyes of the Lord, the Reformed church has a name that it is living, but it is dead.

The Lord reacted to this deadness by raising up a group of believers who were still within Catholicism. They started what is now called mysticism and never left the Roman Catholic Church. Some of the persons were Madame Guyon, Father Fenelon, and Brother Lawrence. Even though this group of seeking ones was within the Catholic Church, they were very much for the inner life. Many who care for the inner life have received help from these mystics. Later, William Law, a British brother, adopted mysticism and improved it. Then Andrew Murray received help from William Law and became a giant in the inner-life line.

However, most Christians do not pay adequate attention to this matter. Teachings are apparent, and gifts are visible; however, the inner life is something mysterious. It is easy for us to talk about our clothing, including our shoes, socks, pants, and shirt. It is also easy for us to talk about our physical body—our hands, feet, nose, eyes, and ears. But it is hard to talk about our physical life, because life is mysterious. We need clothing and we need our body, but without the physical life we simply become a well-dressed person with a beautified body lying in the mortuary. If we do not have the physical life, we are a corpse. Today the situation of Christianity is almost like this: dressing people up and beautifying them yet being short of life.

Some Christians even speak about life, but most of them do not know what they are talking about. They do not know what is life, they do not know who is life, and they do not know how to grow in life. They only have the term *life*. Nearly all preachers, ministers, and speakers know how to quote John 14:6 and John 10:10, which say, "I am the way and the reality and the life," and "I have come that they may have life and may have it abundantly." But if you check with them, asking what is life and how can we grow in life, most would answer that they do not know.

In the practice of the church life, the primary thing to be emphasized is life. Sometimes we are asked by others to tell them what is wrong in their place, but we should never do it. If a person is dead, what is the profit to tell him that he is wrong in this matter or that matter? Even if he could realize, he could not change. But still some try to help the dead ones to have a change. Thirty years ago I did this in my ministry, but not today. At that time I told some people that they were wrong in this and wrong in that and also that they had to have a change. After telling them, I even helped them to have a change, but not today. I have learned that it is of no profit. Our need is to be made alive. When we have life, it takes care of everything. Life will cause people to realize that they need a turn. Then in life they turn by themselves.

In the Lord's recovery of the church life in a certain place, there may be a genuine local church. But without the practicality of life, it will be dead. It may be right in every aspect, but it is dead. The dead body in the mortuary was a real person, but it is now a dead person. Thus, the primary thing in the practicality of the church life is life. We can never be too much for the matter of life. Other things can be overemphasized, but the matter of life can never be overemphasized.

GROWTH IN LIFE

The most significant thing with life is growth. If there is no growth, it means that either there is no life, or there is something wrong. We need to grow in life. In John 6:57 the Lord Jesus said, "He who eats Me, he also shall live because of Me." Do you think that one lives without growing? Look at the young people: they are not only living but also growing.

While one lives, he grows. We must not only live by the Lord but also grow by Him.

The Lord Jesus also told us in John 21:15 that we have to feed the lambs. Put these three verses together from the book of John. It is quite meaningful. "I have come that they may have life and may have it abundantly...He who eats Me, he also shall live because of Me...Feed My lambs." We grow by what we eat, and we also feed others with what we eat. We eat Jesus, so we feed people Jesus. Jesus is food. He is the green pasture, the tender grass for His lambs. We serve His lambs Jesus, not with a mere teaching or doctrine about Jesus. Mere teachings never feed people. We feed the lambs with the element, the ingredient, of Jesus.

This is why we do not like to teach people so much and why we like to ask them to call on the name of the Lord. Mothers do not feed their children with teachings. They do not teach them to grow, but they help them to grow by feeding them. Day by day, three to five times a day, they feed the little ones. Then as a result of being fed, the children get something for their growth. They grow by what they eat. In the church life it is the same. This is not our Christian faith; however, for the proper and adequate practice of the church life, we must have the growth in life.

GROWTH IN LIFE
SOLVING ALL PROBLEMS

If there are some problems among the saints in a local church, the best way to solve the problems is to turn their attention to the matter of feeding, to the matter of growth in life. Medical doctors know that the best medicine is food. If one eats properly and sufficiently, the nourishment from the food will take care of all kinds of disease and weakness. If the saints feed on the Lord Jesus properly, after a certain time all the deadness will be swallowed up by life. Do not ever try to solve a problem by your maneuvering. In politics that might be fine but not in the church. In the church, the more one plays politics, the more he will be deadened. He will first deaden himself and then deaden others. Be honest. Be frank. Be sincere. And never play politics. The only thing that works is the growth in life. Learn to help people grow.

Sometimes strong persons try to influence others. This also should never be done. If you have learned something of the Lord, if you have some measure of growth in life, the Spirit of life will surely honor it and impress people with what you have learned. There is no need for anyone to try to exercise any influence upon others. Eventually, this kind of behavior will create a mess. Learn to be so simple, just living in the spirit and ministering life.

Exercising influence over others is one thing, and ministering life to others is another. To exercise influence over others is still something of man's doing. Let me illustrate in the following way. Suppose I have the experience of life in doing things and have learned to do them all the time in the spirit. All that I should do is simply fellowship with you about this, presenting what I have learned and what I have experienced. Perhaps I can, from the Word, minister something based upon my experience of walking in the spirit. However, if I have the intention to do something with a kind of plan, step by step, this is wrong. I may be able to convince others about this matter. It may even sound quite nice. Some may be convinced that they have to walk in the spirit, but they only pick up the teaching, not the genuine experience of walking in the spirit. If so, I am not ministering life; I am only exercising the influence of my experience upon them. Eventually, this will become a kind of movement. Everybody will talk about how we must walk in life, in the spirit, but it is only talk. There is almost no real walk in the spirit. In the local churches we need to have the genuine growth in life, without any politics and without anyone exercising any influence over others. Our need is that only life would be ministered to others.

LIFE AND GROWTH
IN LIFE IN FIRST CORINTHIANS

Why do I say that the growth in life is the primary

thing in the practicality of the church life? I will refer you to 1 Corinthians. People misuse this book very much. The main thing the Brethren picked up from 1 Corinthians was the teachings. To pick up only the teachings is an inadequate application of the book of 1 Corinthians. The main thing the Pentecostal people picked up from 1 Corinthians was the gifts. This is also a misuse of 1 Corinthians.

Paul says, "I gave you milk to drink" (3:2). Is this teaching? Is this gifts? He also says in 1 Corinthians 13:1, "If I speak in the tongues of men and of angels but do not have love [the expression of life], I have become sounding brass or a clanging cymbal [something that gives sound, but is without life]." Paul says further that when he came to Corinth, he did not come with persuasive words of wisdom, eloquent teaching, but in demonstration of the Spirit (2:4). Then in chapter 14 of 1 Corinthians he says that when he comes to them again, if he comes speaking in tongues, what will he profit them (v. 6). Also, he says that he would rather speak five clear words than ten thousand words in a tongue (v. 19). These verses show us clearly that Paul did not appreciate the teachings or the gifts very much.

However, Paul did appreciate life. In 1 Corinthians after Paul says, "I gave you milk to drink," he says, "I planted, Apollos watered, but God caused the growth." (3:6). He also declares that the last Adam became a life-giving Spirit (15:45) and that he who is joined to the Lord is one spirit (6:17). These verses relate altogether to the matter of life and growth in life. They clearly reveal that the primary practice in the local church is feeding, planting, watering, and growing, with the realization that today Christ is not only a Giver of gifts but a life-giving Spirit. Life is the real practicality. Teachings are for this, and even the gifts are for this. But today most Christians have divorced all the teachings and gifts from life. They care only for teachings or gifts but not life. The normal, proper thing is that we need all the teachings and also the gifts, but we need them for the growth in life.

LIFE AND GROWTH IN LIFE
FOR OUR PRACTICE

Life and growth in life are not our Christian faith, but they are necessities in our practice. If we pay our attention only to teachings and gifts, we are still a local church, but I assure you, either we will be a dead one or a dissenting one. First, we will become dissenting among ourselves, and then we will have a split. We will be deadened, and then we will have a division. Only life and growth in life can keep us alive and keep us in oneness all the time.

When we all turn to our spirit, realizing the need for life and the growth in life and calling on the name of the Lord, love, the uniting power, is there. All the ingredients and elements of Christ will be sweet and nourishing to us. We all will grow together, and none will care to dispute over teachings or impose gifts on others. This is the way for the practice of the church life.

LIFE AND GROWTH IN LIFE
IN EPHESIANS

Paul, in the book of Ephesians, says, "Until we all arrive at...a full-grown man" (4:13)—not a highly-educated man but a full-grown man. Then Paul continues, "That we may be no longer little children...but...may grow up into Him in all things" (vv. 14-15). This book also reveals that life and the growth in life are all we need. The teachings and gifts are at best the means for ministering the nourishing element to people, but they are not the nourishing element itself. For cooking, there are certain utensils, but we do not serve people the utensils. We serve the nourishing element. Gifts and teachings have their place, but the nourishing elements are Christ, the Spirit, and the living word.

If we practice this, we all will grow until we arrive at maturity, at a full-grown man, and no one among us will still be a little child. We will grow up into Him in all things. Even as Ephesians 2:21 says, we will all grow into a temple, into a real building. This is not accomplished by teaching or by the exercise of gifts but altogether by life and the growth in life.

LIFE AND GROWTH IN LIFE
IN FIRST PETER

Peter says that as newborn babes we all have to long for the milk of the word that by it we may grow (1 Pet. 2:2). We will grow by the milk of the word, and then we will become living stones being built up as a spiritual house (v. 5).

A FINAL WORD

I hope that we all will realize that in the normal church life, the proper practice is to pay our full attention to the matter of life and the growth in life. Otherwise, we may be a genuine local church, yet we will be a dead one full of problems. May the Lord be merciful to us. We stand on our Christian faith, but we practice life and the growth in life. This is the first item of the practicality in the local church.

CHAPTER SIX

THE PRACTICALITY OF THE CHURCH LIFE

(2)

Scripture Reading: 2 Cor. 3:17; 2 Tim. 4:22; 1:7; 2:22; 3:16a; 4:3; 1:13; Eph. 6:17-18; Rom. 10:12; 1 Cor. 12:3, 13b; 14:31-32

In the last chapter we saw that life is the primary matter in the practicality of the church life. We need life and growth in life, and for life and growth in life we need the eating of the Lord. Eating results in growth unto a full-grown man. Then, after eating, we must feed the lambs. The issue of all this is the building.

THE EATING OF JESUS

Jesus said, "I am the bread of life...He who eats Me, he also shall live because of Me" (John 6:35, 57). Jesus is the bread of life, but how do we eat this bread? Most Christians know that Jesus is the bread of life, but they do not know *how* to eat Him. Also, they do not know *where* He is, and further, they do not know *what* He is. If we are going to eat something, we first of all need to know the nature, the element, the essence, of the food that we are going to eat. Depending on the nature of the food, we will know what kind of utensil to use in eating. The way we eat something depends on the element, the essence, of the food. Therefore, we need to know *what* Jesus is.

THE SUBSTANCE OF JESUS

What is Jesus? Second Corinthians 3:17 says, "The Lord is the Spirit." This verse tells us not only who Jesus is but also what Jesus is. Jesus is the Spirit. Spirit is His substance, His essence.

To eat Jesus, first of all we must know that He is the Spirit. He is not only God, not only man, not only our Redeemer, not only our Savior, not only our Lord; He is even the Spirit. Some say that Jesus is now in the heavens and that He works in us through the Spirit. Others say that He is *in* the Spirit. However, it is really hard to find some verses in the New Testament which say that Jesus works in us through the Spirit, and there are no verses which say that Jesus is *in* the Spirit. But it is easy to find verses which tell us that Jesus today *is* the Spirit (John 14:16-20; 1 Cor. 15:45; 2 Cor. 3:17). Because many Christians are not clear that today the Lord is the Spirit, they do not know how to eat Him.

In John 6, when the Lord said that He was the bread of life and that they must eat Him, the Jewish disciples were bothered. Some did not understand. So the Lord Jesus answered them, saying, "It is the Spirit who gives life" (v. 63). This indicated that if He was going to be the bread that gives life, He had to be the Spirit. Later He went to the cross, died there, and was resurrected, becoming a life-giving Spirit (1 Cor. 15:45). What is Jesus? He is Spirit.

WHERE JESUS IS

Second Timothy 4:22 clearly tells us *where* the Lord Jesus is. It says, "The Lord be with your spirit." Where is the Lord Jesus today? Praise the Lord for 2 Timothy 4:22! We should never forget this verse. It tells us where the Lord Jesus is today. He is in our spirit. These two spirits, the Lord Jesus as the life-giving Spirit and our spirit, are joined together as one spirit (1 Cor. 6:17).

A STRONG SPIRIT

Then we have the third verse, 2 Timothy 1:7. The spirit we have, our human spirit, is not a spirit of cowardice. It is not a weak spirit but a spirit of power and of love and of sobermindedness.

PURSUING WITH THOSE WHO CALL ON THE LORD

After realizing that we have such a spirit, what shall we

do? There is a fourth verse, 2 Timothy 2:22. It says, "Pursue righteousness, faith, love, peace with those who call on the Lord out of a pure heart." This verse tells us that we should pursue spiritual virtues by calling on Him out of a pure heart. Number one, the Lord Jesus is the Spirit. Number two, He is in our spirit. Number three, our spirit is a spirit that is strong. Number four, we have to pursue with those who call on the Lord out of a pure heart by exercising our spirit.

PRAY-READING THE WORD

Next we have the fifth verse, 2 Timothy 3:16: "All Scripture is God-breathed." The Lord is not only the Spirit within our spirit; He is also the word in the Scripture. Every word in the Bible is His breath. The Scriptures help us to call on the Lord, to breathe the Lord in. The Greek word *pneuma,* translated as "Spirit," also means "breath" or "air" or "wind." Therefore, the Lord Jesus as the Spirit is the breath of life to us. If you know that the Lord Jesus is the Spirit, the breath, it is easy to breathe Him in. One who does not know how to breathe may say that calling on the Lord is too simple. To him, saying, O Lord Jesus! O Lord Jesus! is too simple. However, if he does not like to be so simple, there are sixty-six books that can be used. He can open up to any chapter, to any verse, to any line, and begin to pray. As an example, he may pray, "In the beginning God created. Amen! In the beginning. Oh, in the beginning. Amen! God created. God created the heavens and the earth. Hallelujah!" (Gen. 1:1).

The Bible is a wonderful storehouse. Come to the Scriptures, and pick up all the riches of Christ (Eph. 3:8). Do not come only to read by exercising your mentality. That may dry you up. Along with your reading, you should exercise your spirit to pray what you read. If you will do it, you will surely be filled with the Lord. This is to feed on the Lord. So many can testify that this is true. When you have tasted it, you will never give it up. However, do not insist upon it as an item of our Christian faith.

CALLING AND PRAY-READING
AS THE BEST PRACTICALITY

Romans 10:12 says, "The same Lord is Lord of all and rich to all who call upon Him." How could you enjoy the riches of Christ? The best way is to call upon Him. The Lord is rich to all who call upon Him. At any time, in any kind of situation, simply call, "O Lord Jesus! O Lord Jesus!" Do not try to get yourself delivered out of your circumstances. If you do not know how to answer someone, if you do not know what to do, if you are afraid that you will lose your temper, if you are fearful that you will be tempted, call on the name of the Lord. The Lord is rich to all who call upon Him.

First Corinthians 12:13 says that we "were all given to drink one Spirit." We have been positioned to drink, but how do we drink? In the same chapter, verse 3 says that "no one can say, Jesus is Lord! except in the Holy Spirit." In other words, when you say Lord Jesus, you are in the Holy Spirit. Therefore, we all need to practice saying, "O Lord Jesus." This is the real calling on the Lord. It is not just to pray. It is not just to ask. It is to call upon Him.

Lamentations 3:55-56 says, "I called upon Your name, O Jehovah, / From the lowest pit. / You have heard my voice; do not hide / Your ear at my breathing, at my cry." I like the word, "I called upon Your name...from the lowest pit." Sometimes our dear wives or husbands are our low pit. Out of your low pit, call upon the name of the Lord.

These verses also clearly show us that our crying, our calling on the name of the Lord, is our breathing. In breathing is drinking, and in drinking is eating. When you breathe, you drink; when you drink, you eat. Open yourself from your spirit, and with your mouth call, "O Lord Jesus." It is so sweet, so refreshing, so comforting, and so enlightening. Also, it is so strengthening and even so watering. Then try pray-reading.

These two matters are very practical for the church life. The early believers practiced calling on the name of the Lord. It was evidence that they were followers of Jesus as the church people (Acts 9:14). The apostle Paul, in Ephesians, a book on the church, charged the believers to "receive...the word of God, by means of all prayer" (6:17-18). To receive the word of God by means of prayer is to pray-read the Word. This is for the church to be prevailing against the evil power of Satan, as shown in Ephesians 6.

No one can say that the fact of pray-reading is not in the Bible. One may say that in the Bible there is not such a term as *pray-reading*. Neither is the word *Trinity* in the Bible, but the fact of the Trinity is in the Bible. The fact of pray-reading is also in the Bible. Therefore, we need to receive the word of God by prayer. But do not think that I am teaching this as a part of our Christian faith. I am not teaching calling on the Lord and pray-reading the Bible as the Christian faith, but I am recommending them as the best practicality for the church life.

THE HEALTHY TEACHING

In the Scripture Reading at the beginning of this chapter, we included 2 Timothy 4:3 and 1:13. These verses are concerning the healthy word, the healthy teaching. Why at the end of his ministry did the apostle Paul tell Timothy to take care of the healthy teaching? It was because by that time there were teachings that were not healthy. The King James Version says "sound doctrine" and "sound words" in these verses. Other translations use the words "fundamental teaching" or "fundamental words," but both "sound" and "fundamental" do not adequately express the meaning of the Greek word. The best translation is "healthy." There may be teachings, but these teachings may not be healthy. They do not minister anything of nourishment. We must take care of the healthy teachings.

Health relates to our physical life. We also need some healthy teaching related to our spiritual life. Paul says that the time will come when people will not tolerate the healthy teaching (4:3). They will be like the people of Israel in the wilderness who considered the manna to be too simple. They wanted to eat some garlic and onions from Egypt. They could not bear simple food. This is what Paul meant when he said that the time will come when people will not tolerate the healthy teaching. These will have itching ears, heaping up to themselves teachers upon teachers.

Many of today's Christians have itching ears wanting to hear teachings, but few of these teachings are healthy. We do not need teachings that satisfy itching ears. We need healthy teachings that feed our spirit. Some may ask: "Don't we need some teachings?" Yes we do, but we do not need the kind of teachings that satisfy the itching ears. We need teachings that are healthy, that can nourish our spirit.

The teachings that the Lord has given to His recovery are healthy, full of nourishment. If one does not care for his itching ears but only for his hungry spirit, surely he will appreciate all these teachings. The Lord is the Spirit, the Lord be with your spirit, you have a strong spirit, you have to exercise your spirit to call on the Lord, and you have to pray-read His Word—these are the healthy teachings the Lord has given us for the practice of the church life.

PROPHESYING IN THE MEETINGS

Now I will point out one more thing that is also a part of the practicality of the church life. When I was a young Christian, I was taught that we should not say anything or do anything in a meeting unless we had the inspiration of the Holy Spirit of God. Later, I got to know that the Pentecostal movement told people to pray and wait until something would fall upon them from the heavens. But in 1 Corinthians, concerning the meetings, there is no verse that tells us that we have to get the inspiration of the Holy Spirit before we can function in a meeting. Neither is there a verse in this book that tells us we have to wait until something falls upon us from the heavens. However, 1 Corinthians 14:31 does say, "You can all prophesy one by one." The following verse says, "And the spirits of prophets are subject to prophets." This means that we, as the prophets, have to give the order to our spirit. Suppose you are about to walk. Do you wait for some inspiration? Do you wait until something comes down upon you from the heavens? As living persons, we have two feet. Our feet are subject to us. When it is time to walk, we simply give the order to our feet. When you come to the meeting, or when you are home, or when you are in other places, say something, prophesy, for the Lord. Take the initiative and give the order to your spirit. Exercise your spirit and say something. This is the concept of the Bible, but it is not the concept of the natural man or the religious man. Religiously and naturally, we do not have such a concept. The religious and natural concept is that we have to wait for the Lord's inspiration, or we have to pray and wait until something falls down from the heavens upon us in a miraculous, supernatural way. However, the concept of the Bible is that today the Lord Jesus as the life-giving Spirit is in our spirit (15:45; 2 Tim. 4:22), and we have a strong spirit (1:7). We do not only have a strong spirit; we also have a rich spirit because the Lord who is rich is within our spirit. Now what shall we do? We must prophesy. We must speak something for the Lord. If we believe that the word in 1 Corinthians 14:31 is the word of God, we must receive it and put it into practice. Take the initiative and start to say something for the Lord. Tell your spirit to follow you, and you will have something to say.

Sometimes when we come to the meetings a little tired or even a little lazy, we would ask the Lord to give us a vacation, a rest, from speaking. When we do this, we miss the opportunity. However, many times when we feel tired and have the feeling that we cannot speak anything, there is still a kind of urging within to say something. When it is like this and we speak, that is always the best word. On other occasions, you came to a meeting, thinking you had a word to speak, and spoke it, but the word was a poor one. Why? Because you had to at least exercise your mind a little to remember what you had received that morning. This became a distraction that led you from your spirit to your mind. However, if you feel that you have nothing to say, yet you are urged to speak and do, that will be a wonderful word.

We have a marvelous source within us. We have such a strong spirit, and we have such a rich, divine Spirit within our spirit. This is our capital. When doing business, you need the capital. As Christians, we have billions of dollars worth of capital. Be strong to use it.

A FINAL WORD

Do not consider what I have presented in this chapter as something of our Christian faith. These points are not parts of our Christian faith. However, they are the practicality, even the best practicality, the most profitable practicality, of the church life. They are not required for salvation; they are recommendable for the church practice. I hope that we all will put these points into practice.

CHAPTER SEVEN

THE PRACTICALITY OF THE CHURCH LIFE

(3)

Scripture Reading: John 15:12, 17; Matt. 20:25-27; 23:8-11; 1 Pet. 5:1-3, 5; Rom. 12:4-5; Rev. 1:5b-6a; 5:9b-10a; John 15:5, 8, 16; 21:15b, 16b, 17b; Acts 8:1; 11:19-22

In the last two chapters we have seen that life is the primary thing in the practice of the church life. For the experience and enjoyment of life we need to feed on the Lord Jesus. As we eat, we grow in life, and the issue is the building. We have also seen what the Lord Jesus is, where the Lord Jesus is, and the way to eat Him. The best way to eat Him is to call on His name and pray-read His Word.

In this chapter I will cover eight additional points. These are very practical and strategic for the church life. They are not items of our Christian faith but are necessary things in the practicality of the church life. To be prevailing, a local church must have these items as parts of its practice.

BROTHERLY LOVE

First, we must practice brotherly love (John 15:12, 17). The name *Philadelphia* (Rev. 3:7) means "brotherly love." We have to love one another, yet our love should not be something worldly, emotional, or fleshly. It must be in the spirit, full of the life of Christ. However, we should not spiritualize our love. We have to love from our spirit, but sometimes our love has to be material. If we see a material, physical need of a brother, we should meet that need but not in a worldly way. We must pray and seek the Lord's leading as to the way. The worldly way is to make an open show of our love or to have some self-serving purpose in our love. But the proper brotherly love in the church life has no self-serving purpose and does not make any kind of show.

Suppose a brother is out of a job and does not have any money. Further, he is sick and in need. We should seek the Lord's leading and wisdom as to the way to minister something to meet his need. Many times the Lord will lead us not to let him know that we are offering something to meet his need. We do it in secret. By this way our love helps him and also glorifies the Lord.

Do not love in a fleshly way. Sometimes when the young people do not love someone, they simply do not care for that person. But when they start to love someone, they love in a way that causes damage to others. As an example, one brother may be twenty-one, and the other twenty. They begin to love one another, and as a result, one's shirt and shoes are upon the shoulders and feet of the other. This is a kind of fleshly love. There is no discernment in the spirit and no limitation or restriction. Regardless of how much we love each other, we still must keep a distance of discernment in the spirit and be restricted.

If for some reason a brother needs a shirt or a pair of shoes, we have to love him and do something to meet his need but not in a fleshly way. It must be in the spirit. As we look to the Lord, exercising the discernment in our spirit, He may lead us to place five dollars in an envelope and designate it for the brother. Inside the envelope we may also put a note telling him that the enclosed money is from the Lord to him for purchasing a shirt. Then we put the envelope into the offering box without exposing from whom the gift came. Maybe we type it so that he cannot discern who gave him the gift. The envelope will be given to him by the church, and when he opens it and reads the designation, he will be very much touched by the Lord. To him the five dollars is like manna that came from the heavens. By this way we will never stir up a brother's fleshly gratitude. Genuine love was expressed toward the brother, and it was a glory to the Lord; yet the whole thing was hidden from him. Materially, he could not know who gave him the gift, but spiritually he realized the love of the Lord in the giver towards him. The one receiving the gift senses the love in the Lord of the one giving the gift. This kind of love is pure, yet hidden. It does everything to profit the church and to profit the dear brother. It also glorifies the Lord and does not give the enemy any way to come in and damage anything.

On the other hand, if I am a needy one, I should not let others know my need. In China we had a co-worker who was an elderly sister, the oldest one among us. She always told us not to have a faith that demands others' love. To have such a faith declares that I have faith in God for my living, yet I would let you know how much I need. We should never show our poverty but should do our best to work and earn some money.

If we love others, we should never burden others. Some saints think that because we have brotherly love, there is no need for them to work very much. This is not brotherly love. Brotherly love always takes care of others. It never burdens others. Learn to take care of your own needs by working properly, working hard, and earning something for others.

In the church in Taipei, Taiwan, every Lord's Day and even after some weekday meetings, when the responsible ones open the offering box, there are many envelopes and wrappings with money enclosed. They are designated to a certain sister who is sick in the hospital, or to a brother who needs the tuition for his schooling, or to many others who are in certain needs. All kinds of wrappings are there, yet the people who receive the help do not know who rendered it. Only the Lord knows. This is a basic love.

If this kind of love is practiced, it proves that the church that I am in loves the Lord and that the saints there mean business with the Lord. This kind of love builds. It confirms, strengthens, and unites. As one built up in a local church like this, could I ever be distracted from the church? It is impossible. This is real love. We need love like this, a love that is not expressed in a worldly or fleshly or emotional way, but in the way that is full of the life of the Lord and absolutely in the wisdom of the Spirit. We practice brotherly love, yet we do not know who does this or who does that. We only know that the Lord does it through the saints in the church.

NOT EXERCISING LORDSHIP

In the church no one should exercise lordship. Matthew 20:25-28; 23:8-11; and 1 Peter 5:1-3, 5 reveal that the rulers of the nations exercise lordship over the people, but in the church there is no exercise of lordship. We have the lordship, but it is the lordship of the Lord Himself. No one in the church, regardless of how much responsibility he bears, how much life he ministers to the saints, or how much he has been afforded the Lord's grace for the building up of the local churches, should ever exercise any lordship over others. We all are brothers (Matt. 23:8). We only exercise "brethrenship"; we do not exercise any kind of lordship.

The dear ones who take the lead in all the local churches and all the other brothers and sisters should never consider that there should be anything as a kind of human lordship exercised in the local churches. We do not have any kind of classes in the church life. We only have one class, the brethren. There are no upper and lower classes. I say again, one may be used very much by the Lord and may be full of the Lord's presence, the Lord's life, the Lord's power, and even the Lord's authority, but he should not exercise any lordship over others. To exercise any type of lordship over anyone is absolutely wrong. The Lord Jesus said, "Whoever wants to become great among you shall be your servant" (20:26). The greatest one in the local churches is one who is a servant to all the brothers. We do not exercise lordship, but we do have volunteer slavery. We are not enslaved by anyone, but we like to be a slave to everyone. This is wonderful, and this is the church life. We do not have any human master (23:8). We only have one divine Master, the Lord Jesus.

Neither should we call someone father. To do so absolutely contradicts the Lord's teaching in Matthew 23:9. We have only one Father, our Father in heaven. There are no ranks in the church life. There are no high ones or low ones.

All are on the same level and of the same rank. We all are brothers.

EXERCISING OBEDIENCE

We do not exercise lordship, but we do exercise obedience. We obey one another. In 1 Peter 5:5 the Bible says, "Younger men, be subject to elders." The Bible also says, "Being subject to one another" (Eph. 5:21). Not only the younger ones are subject to the elderly ones; even the elderly ones have to learn subjection. All are subject to one another. This is the balance. One-way traffic always goes to an extreme. We need two-way traffic. As an example, sometimes in a family, the little ones balance the parents. The children might say, "Daddy, why do you sleep so late? Mommy, now is the time for you to go to bed. Mommy, Daddy, why do you talk so much? Mommy, why do you love yourself so much? Why don't you love Daddy? Daddy, don't you see that my uncle needs something?" At times our children are used by the Lord to speak something to us. We parents all need the balance of our children. We should never think, "I am the daddy, so everyone in the family has to listen to me." We all need balance.

In the church life the brothers should never force the sisters to be subject to them. Some brothers in certain so-called local churches have declared to the sisters that based on 1 Corinthians 11:3 they are the head of the women, and all the sisters must be subject to them. Surely this kind of head needs to be balanced. The brothers need the balance from the sisters. We all need to learn something from others. Learn to be subject to others. Without this kind of balance there will be only one-way traffic, and this always leads to an extreme.

In the church I may be one of the local elders, yet I still need to be subject to all the brothers, even to the sisters, and listen to them. All the elders must listen to others' concepts, others' sensations, others' feelings, and others' words. Then they should bring all the fellowship to the Lord and seek the Lord's leading. Maybe the decision will be made not according to what the elders felt but partly according to what the brothers and the sisters feel and partly according to the Lord's revelation. Then the church is kept in balance and can go on in a proper way.

EXERCISING TO FUNCTION

It must be our practice that all the members of the church are functioning members in the Body (Rom. 12:4-5; 1 Cor. 14:24-26, 31-32). It should not be that only a few are the functioning members, and the rest are passive. All must be active members. A serious degradation among Christians is that most of them are passive. Therefore, we must exercise the real Body ministry. Today when people speak about the Body ministry, they consider that two, three, or four ministering is the Body ministry, but the Body ministry is when all the members are functioning. If three hundred meet together, all three hundred must function.

Our body has many parts. When we walk or jump, every part of our body functions; not one part is passive. Every saint must be encouraged to enter into this practice. If we are about to call a hymn, it is better to help a younger one or a weaker one call it. Also we must help all the members to stand up and say something. Perhaps one may only say, "O Lord Jesus"; however, this may be the beginning of his functioning.

On the other hand, some are too active. These need to give opportunity to others and become active in helping others to function.

THE UNIVERSAL PRIESTHOOD

We also need to practice the universal priesthood (Rev. 1:6; 5:10), which means that every believer is a priest. In the practice of the church life, we should not have clergy or laymen but only priests. In the Body of Christ we are members, and in the service to God the Father we are priests. Therefore, we not only must function in the meetings; we also must serve. In the church there is much service, and everyone should take part in these services. Be a serving priest, not just a functioning member. We all must practice this.

ENDEAVORING TO BEAR FRUIT

In the church life we all need to bear fruit. The Lord Jesus said, "I chose you, and I set you that you should go forth and bear fruit and that your fruit should remain" (John 15:16). This is not solely to have the outreach by preaching the gospel. Nor is it only to have "soul winning." It is to impart life to others. In Matthew 28:19, Mark 16:15, and Luke 24:47 we are told to go and preach, but in the Gospel of John we are told to go and bear fruit. The Gospel of John is a book on life; therefore, the preaching, the outreach, in this book is the impartation of life to others, causing them to become fruit.

Never say that numbers do not mean anything. In Acts 11:21 the divine record says, "A great number...believed." If numbers do not mean anything, the Holy Spirit would never have said this. In married life we need children. If after a long period of time, a married couple does not have children, this indicates that something is wrong. Also the bringing forth of children is simply to impart the life we have into our children.

We also need some spiritual children. We need to impart our spiritual life into our spiritual children. If the local church in a certain place has fifty this year, the next year fifty-one, the third year forty-nine, and the fourth year forty-five, the church should not try to vindicate itself by saying that it does not care for numbers but only for quality. A local church needs numbers. Although in a spiritual sense, some members who are brought forth may be crippled, blind, deaf, or lame, it is still good. In appearance it may be a mess, but it is better than nothing, and something will come out of it. Physically, some lame fathers have brought forth very strong sons.

All local churches must encourage every brother and sister to produce. All the saints must endeavor to bring forth fruit, even remaining fruit. Do not be troubled thinking that if we bring forth many, the church cannot take care of them, and some will die. Perhaps this is true, but some will remain, and this is better than nothing. Every marriage that is normal produces children. We have to stress this very much and put it into practice.

FEEDING THE LAMBS

The next point is the feeding of the lambs (John 21:15-17). Bearing fruit is one thing; feeding the lambs is another. If we are proper, on one hand, we bring many unbelievers to the meetings and, on the other hand, we take care of several new believers. We have to bear fruit, and we also have to feed the lambs. In these two matters we should not be special or particular. The church is for everyone, including the young people, the middle-aged ones, and the older ones. The church is for all kinds of people. We do not know from what direction the Lord will bring people into the church. While Peter was suffering persecution in Jerusalem, he might have thought that Saul of Tarsus surely was going to hell. But beyond Peter's expectation, the Lord turned Saul into an apostle.

The church is not built up with the persons we intend to have but with the persons God has chosen before the foundation of the world (Eph. 1:4). We cannot predict whether our children, our parents, our cousins, our schoolmates, or our neighbors will be the church people. Only the Lord knows. We just go in a general way according to the Lord's leading and bear fruit. Do not do anything special, strange, or peculiar, and do not classify people. The Lord may even raise up some good saints from the opposing ones. Who will be saved, who will be the elders, who will be the spiritual ones, only the Lord knows. It is not up to us; it is up to Him. Yet we still have to do our duty to bear fruit and feed the lambs. This is not your work, nor my work, nor even our work; it is the Lord's work.

SPREADING BY MIGRATION

In Acts 8:1 we see that persecution came against the church in Jerusalem, thus scattering the saints and forcing them to migrate. Acts 11:19 shows that the scattered ones preached the gospel as they went, and some local churches were raised up. Reports went back to the church in Jerusalem, and it sent Barnabas to have fellowship with them (v. 22). The spreading of the gospel and the church life in the first century began by the migration of the saints. The going out of the apostles began from Antioch (13:1-3).

Therefore, a good number of the saints in the local churches should be migrating ones; first migrating from city to city, and state to state within this country, and then migrating to other countries. For the sake of the Lord's recovery, we should not be narrow-sighted and only set our eyes on the local church in the city where we reside. We need a larger view.

The more a church gives up people for migration, the more people it gets. The more a church keeps, the more it loses. Do not try to keep people. Do your best to give them for the Lord's spread. Do not be narrow-sighted, thinking you will lose something. You will never lose. Even if you lose on this earth, surely you will gain in the heavens. Praise the Lord for the way of migration!

A FINAL WORD

None of the points that we have covered in the last three chapters are aspects of our Christian faith. However, all of them should be put into practice; otherwise, a local church could never be strong and prevailing. If all these points are put into practice, a local church will become strong and prevailing. These are not items of our Christian faith, but they must become part of the practicality of the church life.

ABOUT THE AUTHOR

Witness Lee was born in 1905 in northern China and raised in a Christian family. At age 19 he was fully captured for Christ and immediately consecrated himself to preach the gospel for the rest of his life. Early in his service, he met Watchman Nee, a renowned preacher, teacher, and writer. Witness Lee labored together with Watchman Nee under his direction. In 1934 Watchman Nee entrusted Witness Lee with the responsibility for his publication operation, called the Shanghai Gospel Bookroom.

Prior to the Communist takeover in 1949, Witness Lee was sent by Watchman Nee and his other co-workers to Taiwan to ensure that the things delivered to them by the Lord would not be lost. Watchman Nee instructed Witness Lee to continue the former's publishing operation abroad as the Taiwan Gospel Bookroom, which has been publicly recognized as the publisher of Watchman Nee's works outside China. Witness Lee's work in Taiwan manifested the Lord's abundant blessing. From a mere 350 believers, newly fled from the mainland, the churches in Taiwan grew to 20,000 in five years.

In 1962 Witness Lee felt led of the Lord to come to the United States, and he began to minister in Los Angeles. During his 35 years of service in the U.S., he ministered in weekly meetings and weekend conferences, delivering several thousand spoken messages. Much of his speaking has since been published as over 400 titles. Many of these have been translated into over fourteen languages. He gave his last public conference in February 1997 at the age of 91.

He leaves behind a prolific presentation of the truth in the Bible. His major work, *Life-study of the Bible,* comprises over 25,000 pages of commentary on every book of the Bible from the perspective of the believers' enjoyment and experience of God's divine life in Christ through the Holy Spirit. Witness Lee was the chief editor of a new translation of the New Testament into Chinese called the Recovery Version and directed the translation of the same into English. The Recovery Version also appears in a number of other languages. He provided an extensive body of footnotes, outlines, and spiritual cross references. A radio broadcast of his messages can be heard on Christian radio stations in the United States. In 1965 Witness Lee founded Living Stream Ministry, a non-profit corporation, located in Anaheim, California, which officially presents his and Watchman Nee's ministry.

Witness Lee's ministry emphasizes the experience of Christ as life and the practical oneness of the believers as the Body of Christ. Stressing the importance of attending to both these matters, he led the churches under his care to grow in Christian life and function. He was unbending in his conviction that God's goal is not narrow sectarianism but the Body of Christ. In time, believers began to meet simply as the church in their localities in response to this conviction. In recent years a number of new churches have been raised up in Russia and in many European countries.

OTHER BOOKS PUBLISHED BY
Living Stream Ministry

Titles by Witness Lee:

Abraham—Called by God	978-0-7363-0359-0
The Experience of Life	978-0-87083-417-2
The Knowledge of Life	978-0-87083-419-6
The Tree of Life	978-0-87083-300-7
The Economy of God	978-0-87083-415-8
The Divine Economy	978-0-87083-268-0
God's New Testament Economy	978-0-87083-199-7
The World Situation and God's Move	978-0-87083-092-1
Christ vs. Religion	978-0-87083-010-5
The All-inclusive Christ	978-0-87083-020-4
Gospel Outlines	978-0-87083-039-6
Character	978-0-87083-322-9
The Secret of Experiencing Christ	978-0-87083-227-7
The Life and Way for the Practice of the Church Life	978-0-87083-785-2
The Basic Revelation in the Holy Scriptures	978-0-87083-105-8
The Crucial Revelation of Life in the Scriptures	978-0-87083-372-4
The Spirit with Our Spirit	978-0-87083-798-2
Christ as the Reality	978-0-87083-047-1
The Central Line of the Divine Revelation	978-0-87083-960-3
The Full Knowledge of the Word of God	978-0-87083-289-5
Watchman Nee—A Seer of the Divine Revelation ...	978-0-87083-625-1

Titles by Watchman Nee:

How to Study the Bible	978-0-7363-0407-8
God's Overcomers	978-0-7363-0433-7
The New Covenant	978-0-7363-0088-9
The Spiritual Man • 3 volumes	978-0-7363-0269-2
Authority and Submission	978-0-7363-0185-5
The Overcoming Life	978-1-57593-817-2
The Glorious Church	978-0-87083-745-6
The Prayer Ministry of the Church	978-0-87083-860-6
The Breaking of the Outer Man and the Release ...	978-1-57593-955-1
The Mystery of Christ	978-1-57593-954-4
The God of Abraham, Isaac, and Jacob	978-0-87083-932-0
The Song of Songs	978-0-87083-872-9
The Gospel of God • 2 volumes	978-1-57593-953-7
The Normal Christian Church Life	978-0-87083-027-3
The Character of the Lord's Worker	978-1-57593-322-1
The Normal Christian Faith	978-0-87083-748-7
Watchman Nee's Testimony	978-0-87083-051-8

Available at
Christian bookstores, or contact Living Stream Ministry
2431 W. La Palma Ave. • Anaheim, CA 92801
1-800-549-5164 • www.livingstream.com